RHYME TYME

The Writing and Musings of James L Baird

James L. Baird

authorHOUSE®

AuthorHouse™
1663 Liberty Drive
Bloomington, IN 47403
www.authorhouse.com
Phone: 1-800-839-8640

First published by AuthorHouse 07/18/2011

ISBN: 978-1-4567-3687-3 (sc)
ISBN: 978-1-4567-3689-7 (ebk)
ISBN: 978-1-4567-3690-3 (hc)

Library of Congress Control Number: 2011902720

Printed in the United States of America

Acknowledgment

I wish to express my sincere appreciation to my step-granddaughter Debra Schowengerdt of Waterford, WI, whose untiring efforts and support contributed so immeasurably to the formulation of this work.

Thank You – Thank You

'Grandpa' Jim

A Tribute to Motherhood
(Dedicated to my mother,
nee Sarah Elizabeth 'Sweet' Griffith)

I so often remember my Mother

Who taught us to love one another

Were it father, sister, or brother

It always included all other

We were told of the ways we should share

While she tended our needs with such care

    Now when Gabriel his last tone does blare

I'm sure that my Mom will be there

One Thought for the Day

Why do we so worry and fret

When our time to expire is not yet

Why not smile and thus we'll abet

    All our good fortunes, 'Lest we Forget'

A Real Picker-Upper

If at times you are forlorn or weary

    And your eyes may become a bit teary

    One need not feel down-cast or dreary

Just go and see Harry O'Leary

(Our God also says 'Not to Fear Ye')

There is a Place where Love Dwells

There is a place where Love dwells
Through-out our life-long days
    The place where the Prince of Peace quells
All of our fearful ways

There is a place where Love dwells
It was there right from the start
The place where only truth tells
It's deep within one's heart

The Big Q?

Do we willingly share of our love
    Which is given from heaven above
    Or do we need a reversal of heart
    Ere our love we can freely impart

Won't You Enter My Home

Won't you enter my home, said the fly
As he nodded to all passersby
You may bring all your troubles along
We'll sort out the right from the wrong

Won't you enter my home, said the fly
As he greeted an old passerby
I'll offer my help, said the fly
It may not be much, but I'll try

Over-Eaters Anonymous

While eating my breakfast one morning
My lack of weight loss I was mourning
The reason for which was enjoining
So then, I dieted on dishes by Corning
I lost all the fat with no worth
That contributed so much to my girth

I Met a Man One Day
(Dedicated to my father, Lewis Collins Baird)

I met a man one day

When I was going my way

One whose hair and whose temples were gray

Yet a cheerful 'Good morning' he'd say

Then by chance, it was later that day

When I met the same man on my way

His hair and his temples were gray

Yet a heart-felt 'How are you' he'd say

Now as we went forth on our way

It was nearing the end of the day

There is one thing for sure I can say

It simply is, I met a man that day

A Toast- not a Roast
Georgetown, KY 1972
40th year reunion- classes of 1932, 1933

Here's to the Grads of Ole Garth High
Who've assembled here from both far and nigh
To re-new old friendships and perhaps heave a sigh
As we pause to reflect over coffee and pie

Many years have gone by since last we did dine
But not for the ladies, past thirty-nine!
'Tho fewer Buffalo roam in your land and mine
They'll always be first, just like Auld Lang Syne

And to our dedicated teachers, who with patience supreme
Were ever at hand to encourage each dream
With results so fulfilling, one could hardly but beam
For a 'job so well done' is the name of the theme

And now as we go forward, thru the Autumn of Life
May we tend to discount its stress and its strife
And be ever more thankful, and sound with our fife
All praises to God, the Creator of Life

Contributed by James Lewis Baird
President, class of 1932

James L. Baird

The Vagaries of Composition

Someday when you're soaking up tan

This rhyme you're prompted to scan

While these lines they are meant to peruse

They sometimes can also amuse

We Love a Parade

I was thoroughly enjoying the parade

    While the Mayor, he looked on from the shade

The drum major led the big band

And his chest it did really expand

Then just as his high-step was made

He was showered with cold lemonade

Are You Lonely at Night

Do you find yourself lonely at night
    When the moon and the stars are so bright
Are you longing to do what is right
Or merely to say that you might

Do you find yourself lonely at night
And you're seeking relief from this plight
If your prayers they are truly contrite
Then you need not feel lonely this night

A Gift to Forget

I herewith present you more verse
Whose content may seem a bit terse
If your reaction is somewhat adverse
    Be assured that the rest are much worse

Tempus Fugit

When we were all young and aspiring
And our efforts they were so untiring
    We pursued wealth, good health and longevity
Unaware that our lives had such brevity

The Masked Lady

I once knew a fencer named Spencer

Who required a long while to convince her

    That her bouts they were all thrust and parry

And so oft' times they could be oh so scary

It's Up 2U
a.k.a. Left Foot Forward

Here's to my Doc, Stanley Gruhn

Who loves a really good tune

    Yet if he is to dance well, however

It surely must be now or never

Whoa Boy

    There was a young sprinter named Murray

Who tore down the street in a hurry

'Midst all of the hustle and bustle

Just walking became quite a tussle

In the crowd he did cause such a flurry

That he got from them all the razzberry

While Sitting Alone at the Bar

It was right after leaving my car
That I crossed the street to the bar
No matter the time or just when
I'm sure it was called "The Cruise Inn"

While sitting alone at the bar
I met my good friend Kurt Millar
We both said 'hello' and were thirsty
    We made known both our names, but first he
Introduced his beautiful daughter, Miss Kirsti

Now Kurt's hair, it did seem a bit sandy
And his generous smile was a dandy
It was while sitting alone at the bar
That I first met my friend Kurt Millar

Hope Springs Eternal

There was an older Lady named Halliday
Who strove to continue her younger way
    But with all of her ailments and maladies
She never came close to her salad days

Calling Dr. Einstein

There was this older man from Duluth
Who was wont to recall of his youth
But then ageing became his concern
A process in which we all take our turn
Now growing older, it may only be relative
    Especially when considering the alternative!

Diet Unchanged

    There was once a Lady named Toodles
Who craved to eat oodles of noodles
When offered a serving of strudels
Said, away with it all, I'll have noodles

What's Got Got to Do With It?
So much for contraction

When we're continually watching TV
The constant use of 'We've Got' you'll see
Of the weather we're waiting to hear
    Of course we know what 'We've Got' right here
When we're told 'We've Got' weather real nice
Just the two words 'WE HAVE' would suffice

Hello Out There!

There was once a mariner named Hathaway
    Whose schooner went down near an isle far away
And 'tis a sad thing that we have to say
Lived the rest of his life as a castaway

Not in My Court Old Chap
a.k.a. Gavel down- moving right along

    In London lived a Magistrate named Crockett
With a heavy case load on his docket
To criminals he was well known to sock it
For his boat, no one e'er dared to rock it
Ere the Barristers' defense was composed
The Magistrate declared the 'case closed'

Without Parallel
a.k.a. 'Nokum Harrison'

When at times I'm inclined to reflect

And my thinking it is circumspect

For one name I've the greatest respect

Just to think how horrendous the cost

Were it e'er that we should have lost

The priceless poetry of our Legend Bob Frost

Waddle-Waddle
w/a verse-less ending

When wondering just how long it had been

Since the ducks had flown back to the fen

Their little ducklings walked ever so softly

    Simply because that they couldn't walk hardly

The Ayes Have It
a.k.a. Clarity of Vision
(Dedicated to Dr. John Downing)

Good morning to you Dr. D.

And just how is it you'd be

With your help we all soon will see

    And then we'll shout out with such glee

Depart Not From My Regimen
a.k.a. Over There

My doctor wrote me a prescription

In writing that defied all description

The medication that he did dispense

'Twas all at the patient's expense

The capsules and pills were so numerous

That I found it all a bit humorous

Were I required to take this prescription

    I'd much rather have dealt with conscription

Step Up to the Plate

    There once was a manager named Vince

Who was woefully short on defense

When asked why his offense was hot

Merely said that his defense was not

Homestead Re-visited

When planning a vacation this year
We realized that the time was quite near
So as soon as the school year was out
My family they picked out a route
By my family home-place we'd go
A place that I once had loved so
'Tho the old home, it had long since burned
'Twas to recall how it was that I yearned
The earth had caved in 'round the well
Taking with it the old dinner bell
    The smoke-house which had served us so well
We now found to be merely a shell
Next we observed the old hen-house
Where all was quiet as a mouse
And the only movement we saw
Came from an old crow with no caw
When finished, we all felt it was meant
To be the summer of our discontent

A Woman's Prerogative
a.k.a. Change of Mind

There was this young singer named Nola

Who was wont to drink much Coca-Cola

In Venice, while touring in a gondola

Also listened to her new Motorola

When suddenly she threw out her Cola

Being inspired by her new Motorola

Having had much too much of her Cola

Just stood up and sang Amapola!

Meteorology 101

On a sweltering mid-summer eve

I was anxiously seeking reprieve

From the heat which I scarce could believe

So I finally just rolled up each sleeve

Haberdasher Wanted
a.k.a. Sartorial Non-Excellence

When waiting alone all the while

I was prompted this hour to smile

'Tho our life, it was easy to see

That it was ne'er again to be

Like the Scot who had lived in Dundee

    He had a brogue and wore a kilt that was plaid

When told his whole get-up was sad

Took off in a big huff and got mad

How Sweet It Is

There was once a humming bird named Hector

Who was e'er in quest of more nectar

One Lady-bird, he had just flown past her

As his wings, they beat faster and faster

    'Tho during some of his days there was laughter

'Twas e'er more nectar he was after

Hoist Our Flag to Full Mast
a.k.a. Let's All Bless America

'Tho at times we are prone to complain
That relief from our taxes is in vain
'Tho the price of gas can cause pain
We've incomes most high in the main
'Tho some in this world would destroy
The fabric of our Beloved Old Glory
    There's naught on this earth that equates
With the Living in these United States

Endowment

I suppose, when using hind-sight
    'Twould be some semblance of verse I'd write
With the hope that some people would like
This too, I guess I've known since a tyke

On this earth, it is long that I've been
The Good Lord, He has told me just when
Were the times I should take up my pen
And recount days thru which I had been

My Lord, He has given me these powers
So when someone like You reads or scours
Need not count the days or the hours
One needs only to know that they're OURS

James L. Baird

Return to John 3:16

Remember that no matter what has been our behavior

One need only accept Jesus Christ as their Savior

But to follow our Bible and join in adoption

For salvation we surely have no other option

Reward Forthcoming

When the time comes for inner reflection

And our thoughts can't escape detection

Just remember it is that God's judgment

May be dealt out by His Son that He sent

For those living in every nation

They have e'er sought Eternal Salvation

We need only accept Jesus Christ as our Saviour

No matter what's been our behaviour

For He shouldered all of the world's sin

That's just what He did at the end

Now as life draws near to its end

And we've been forgiven all sin

How comforting to know that is when

We'll all be as One with Him then

To which, we'll all say a resounding AMEN

Billy Graham

Were I to be given but one voice

And should I be granted a choice

I'm sure the whole world will rejoice

    In the future as they still hear your voice

Bethany

(Dedicated to Bethany Joan Schowengerdt,
MARTIN LUTHER High school class of 2008, GREENDALE, WI)

Were I e'er requested, a toast to narrate

'Twould be to Bethany, my step great-granddaughter by fate

One who excels in SOCIAL STUDIES, to mention just one

As she presses onward with her life choice just begun

May our LOVING LORD JESUS, attend her closely always

And e'er be beside her, through-out the length of her days

Euphonious

When one thinks of all the poetry and verse
    Which require all of one's attention to rehearse
And 'tho one strives to mimic o'er time
May it ne'er displace one's effort to rhyme.

Revelation

When 'tis that we've been told, to love one another
Be it one's Father, Mother, Sister or Brother
Should we but pause, and give tho't to life's meaning
    'Tis at last, the reason for one's being, we'll be seeing

Solidarity
a.k.a. Community

When envisioning the spectre of our world living together
We realize 'tis no longer a question of whether
For unless 'tis As One that we All do stand
We might as well our entire society disband

Love One Another

Should it be, we all wonder why we're here in this world?

And our being here seems not to have been herald

If we're sincerely in quest of those acts most vital

One needs only to conform to this verse's title

For when life's mission on earth 'tis through

And we know we've done the best we could do

There is naught more e'er to be asked for than

Having been kind to and e'er mindful of our fellow-man

Tolerance

Tho' in life, we may encounter those we dislike

And association with them, we'd prefer to strike

    Tho' they may be marked by pretense and bombast

May we e'er refrain from an aspersion, to cast

Beneath the Surface

Should I e'er, due to my own fault, fail to mention the
Incomparable Ones I've been privileged to know near a century
Aside from our family, countless other relatives & friends
I've found that the depth of my fellow-man has no ends

A Hoot in the Boot

In Italy there lived a Comic named Nolaff
Who struggled tirelessly to make his audience laugh
Further, in his pre-occupation, he committed a gaffe
For he completely over-looked the balcony riff-raff
Thus when his inappropriate punch line was emitted
He was soundly clobbered with ripe olives not pitted

Change
a.k.a. Non Status Quo

Of the many questions I've been asked off-hand
The most subtle were those that demand
That ere our life's pattern can change
We must all of our thoughts re-arrange
And so, it has e'er been my earnest decision
To give words to this ultimate revision

Things Left Undone

When prone to reflect on the incidents in my life
I discovered they included both love and strife
And 'tho, in an effort to do what was right
I felt that their doing somehow left my sight
'Twas then that I became emotionally distraught
Realizing the countless things of life that I ought

Self Analysis

When defining the nature of compassion & forbearance
We find we're confronted with both patience & tolerance
For 'tis through these virtues that we have the proclivity
To evaluate the degree of one's sensitivity

No Place like Home

And so, just what'll it be for today
Would you prefer to go out or to stay?
Are you bored with the hum-drum of home
And desirous of elsewhere to roam
Then, after experiencing all this diversity outside
And all the hype that may have been implied
You find that compared to a fire-place and good tome
There is no place that can equal your own quiet home

Unlikely Event

We pray that we may ne'er wake up some morn
To find that most vestiges of life are shorn
'Tho such a catastrophe would surely amaze us
Such a happening should ne'er otherwise faze us

Individuality

Should it e'er have been that we were all of one mold
'Twould have been a drab world for one to behold
For 'tis our varied talents and actions most rife
That inherently distinguish us from other elements of life
And ere we're inclined to store our behaviour on shelves
Just be thankful that we were all created as ourselves

Origin

When pondering how it is, that our world came to be
We find that the answer is most difficult to see
For 'tis in our thoughts there are countless questions to beg
Such as which came first, the chicken or the egg?
After exhausting our search for the title of this verse
The answer is that our God created the Universe

Brevity

When confronted with all the things to be done
And they number everything under the sun
Then ere life's quest it is run
You realize that 'tis hardly begun

Opposition

Have you e'er felt yourself betrayed in this world
And 'tis as if your every move is imperiled
Then's the time to summon tho'ts that are uncurled
And counter all that which toward you is hurled

Legal Mumbo-Jumbo
a.k.a. All Rise

If per chance you find yourself required to litigate
And your not guilty plea you're striving to mitigate
If your claim 'tis that you were ne'er near Watergate
Then you'd better have the witnesses to substantiate

Comparison
a.k.a. Infinite Love or the Cross-Bearer

Should we e'er question as to why we were born

One might well remember Him who wore the thorn

    'Twas God's sacrifice, as His Son labored up Calvary's hill

May we ne'er forget, 'twas a promise He did fulfill

When considering all of life's streams we must ford

Surely nothing compares with the Love of our Lord

Dreams

The accomplishment of dreams has e'er been one's hope

Yet to realize this goal, one needs to know of its scope

For all too often, 'tis the hardships, set-backs and no toil

That once again, prove to be the factors to spoil

Added, the limit-less visions of our youth when young

For 'tis the in-completion of all this, time has wrung

Thus, when our life ends with dreams not be-got

We must trust in our God, and be resigned to our lot

Dream On

You may think this one o'er, at your will

When your tho'ts they are placid and still

Tho' your age now may be o'er the hill

    'Tis your dreams, they're ne'er too late to fulfill

Prayer

'Twas one day when I was musing along the way

I pondered o'er the countless things for which I might pray

While aware that my humble rhyming could ne'er e'er say

An adequate thank You for all Your gifts, to this day

'Tis the priceless gift of Your Son Jesus, which mere words can't extol

For thru Him lays the way for the very Salvation of one's Soul

'Twas then tho'ts reverted to my fellow-man

Realizing he's the one ranked highest in His plan

My Health

One day when reviewing my life's derailments
I was struck by the plethora of my ailments
Firstly, 'twas the matter of my ankle edema
Possibly begun when on the out-skirts of Lima
While attempting my lower appendages to hide
    Dr. Gruhn cured with Furosemide & Potassium Chloride
Next appeared one that almost escaped detection
For in my throat was found a yeast infection
My appointment was handled as an emergency
Having come on like a rebel insurgency
And ere I should drink at least one Manhattan
Dr. Cervantes cleared up by prescribing Nystatin
'Twas most lately, I developed cancer in my left ear
Tho' only a basal cell type that I need not fear
And yet, I'd be remiss, should I fail to mention
'Tis that I experienced a modicum of apprehension
So, at age 95, these on-sets were no big surprise
For I'm in relatively good health otherwise

No Qualification

When contemplating any rhymes that are sought
We're faced with many possibilities that we ought
To convey all the very best of our thought
    For lest we lose the meaning and end up with naught
The answer 'tis the Love that our God hath wrought

Life's Components

We know our family consists of Parents, Sisters & Brothers
And 'tis we love and cherish them all like no others
Then when children & grandchildren our lives do complete
As if our God arranged this cycle so replete
Add to this another Component, which exceeds every plan
When we've been kind to & e'er respectful of our fellow-man

Major No-Noes

Of all evil things with which we are cursed
Man's in-humanity to man is the worst
So thus eradicate this evil, we must
    Along with others, such as greed, gluttony, & lust

Do Not Enter

'Twas one day that I met this stranger in Alaska

Who, incidentally, had just arrived from Itasca

From the out-set, we both had rapport, should one ask ya

Thus such was our relation, as we topped our burger with tobasco

Now, 'twas just after completing a round of the pubs

That we encountered a Mother Grizzly and her three Cubs

Tho' well fortified with a liquid not drunk from a box

'Twas a meeting that chilled us, all the way down to our Sox

While staring transfixed at this monstrous Grizzly

Our next course of action came to us quite dizzily

For ere we noted all the fenced-in area there

Too late, we discovered this sign which read FOR BEAR

Unfortunate Encounter

One day I met a vile man most abhorrent

    Upon whom condemnation fell like a torrent

For his un-thinkable acts of aggression

And persistently, despite all his confessions

He did truly surpass all transgressions

Money Talks

There once lived this miserly hermit so morose

That he seemed everything in life to oppose

He held a secret that was of such magnitude

That, understandably, not once did he dare allude

    However, when offered a million bucks to disclose

He spilled his guts, all the way down to his toes

Another Prayer
a.k.a It's a Keeper

Again, when considering a choice of my 'druthers

My-inner tho'ts are drawn to thinking of others

Mindful of all the varied factors that our life covers

'Tis through Creation that we're all Sisters and Brothers

Aware that for disobedience of His commandments we'll pay

When at last, we all come face to face with Him one day

May our Maker forgive the errors of our way

For 'tis for this that I will forever pray

Humanity in Need

When being apprised of all the world's hunger
I was reminded of my childhood when younger
For 'twas oft' that our life failed to meet
The essentials that our being needed to eat
Our prayer, 'tis that our help to our fellow-man
Will, in some small way, conform to His plan
    And lest one's e'er tempted, this rhyme to mock
Think this one o'er, For He Shall Feed His Flock

Friendship

(Dedicated to the Memory of Jefferson Davis Kirkpatrick)

When 'tis that you've just gone to bed
And many tho'ts are rambling 'round in your head
There's one that persists above many to attend
What a treasure to have been blessed with one True Friend

Repentance

    When reflecting on all of one's actions, 'tis one might
Tend to minimize the true nature of their blight
Yet, if we pray for forgiveness and are contrite
'Tis then that one's redemption's in sight

Virtue
a.k.a. Never an Issue

When the counting of one's virtues we attempt
Of course, there's compassion as opposed to contempt
And ere one feels misunderstood and berates
May forgiveness be not the least of one's traits
Tho' impatience may sometimes occur, for instance
We pray one finds one's full share of tolerance
And ere one is prone to complain of one's help-lessness
One might well give consideration to one's self-lessness
Further, lest one's actions attest to one's blindness
May one e'er live a life filled with kindness
Then 'tis in Communion one partakes of the Chalice
When one should ne'er think of greed, envy or malice
Finally, the inexorable presence of His Love does emerge
And 'tis with THIS, that all other virtues converge

Academia Limited

When one is inclined to assess one's own mortality
And becomes aware that 'tis fraught with finality
One gropes tirelessly for a solution to explain
Why 'tis one can't all of our life's answers name
Notwithstanding every iota of knowledge, e'er known to man
'Tis infinitely more that has e'er been encompassed in His plan

It's Worth a Try

Dear Lord, we know Thou art the One of creation

One whose gift could ne'er receive adequate acclamation.

Then why is it then, that we can't as a nation

Simply excuse one's mis-direction, and put on probation

Intent

And now, in a confession, lest I tend to pretend

    'Tis that I've been, one who'd ne'er a mountain ascend

Yet when laboring up the slopes of Mt Everest

My climbing skills, they were put to a test

And I pray that 'tis through my efforts to rhyme

One discovers the meaning of my rhyme, in time

Love

'Tho we may have many concepts of Love

This age-less gift, 'twas giv'n from above

    And tho' o'er time, one may be reluctant to admit it

Just what it is, that age has to do with it

Eternally Paternally

When one contritely seeks the answer to Prayer
One e'er feels assured that 'twill come from up There
And all will be well if one only lays one's soul bare
Yet we find a world rife with pretext, strife, and pother
And all too oft', 'tis that we seem not to bother
    To confess our sins to our Dear Lord Jesus & His Father

Heal Thyself

If, during our life-time, one is healthy throughout
We give end-less thanks for what 'twas all about
And forbid one should e'er be afflicted with gout
    'Tis that one's earnest prayers will cure, leave no doubt

At A Loss to Describe

When, in an effort to determine the destiny of one,
I'm somehow confronted with the battles not won
Tho' one has striven to do what one felt morally right
One was at a loss, 'til these last two lines came in sight
His Love surpasses all extremities known to abound
    And the Salvation of one's Soul, 'tis at last to be found

Naught to Compare

When one finds oneself in deepest concentration
One is confronted with one's eternal salvation
And ere we're judged on the life that we've liv'n
We fervently pray that our sins are forgiv'n
    Should this but happen, from His throne up above
'Twould be yet, another sign of His Infinite Love

Ultimate Appeal

When one thinks of the many intricacies in our life
And of the countless faux-pas that are rife
One need only account for those which are their own
When they've overcome any accusations that are sown
    And when 'tis there's any mis-fortune, that one be-falls
'Tis on the Omnipotence of our Lord that one calls

The Hereafter

When 'tis Eternal Life that we all look toward
And we pray that all our fellow-ones are aboard
For no matter what we may ask of our Lord
'Twill be a request that, at times, we may ill-afford
    Yet, 'tis the assurance of Your Love, needless to say
That has been the crux of our lives, all the way

Contrition

Were I somehow able to recount, all of the actions in my life
Thankfully, 'twould include some ill-doings not too rife
Thus, with these transgressions and weaknesses out-layed
'Tis for their remission and His forgiveness, I've e'er prayed

Damon Runyon's Bailiwick

One day at the track, I met a rail-bird named Kirby
Who claimed to have won every major race 'cept The Derby
Further, he confided, that when walking his trio of Spaniels
He'd sneak a big swig from his flask of Jack Daniels
Thus fortified, he bet a grand on Slow Motion at 100 to 1
'Twas then he passed out completely when that nag WON

'Tis a Giv'n

When, in humility, one is faced with the need of forgiving
No matter whether it be Christmas, Easter, or Thanksgiving
If one's to name the greatest virtue, near the end of one's living
'Tis that one's self and one's love one's still giving

Cloning Not Excluded

Should you but hark to the whole of your heart
You'd realize just why a very special person thou art
Tho' there may be many others who bear your name
And still more individuals who lay claim to fame
Just remember, ere a duplicate you're inclined to proclaim
That, in the order of things, our God created no two beings the
same

Penniless

I once met an inventor, who dreamed of a project so complete
That 'twould render all other modern counterparts obsolete
Tho' to many, he appeared to be a self-professed pundit
Yet all he had e'er lacked, 'twas the wherewithal to fund it

A Far Cry from Reality

When a man boasts endlessly of his flawless behavior

As if it compared favorably with that of our Savior

For when none need not one moment this braggart's claim to digest

'Tis that he may well have his own words to ingest

Without Borders

If one's disturbed o'er the in-flux of immigrants

Who as workers, many are classified as itinerants

In an effort to improve their family's standard of living

They seek work in our country, and of their talents they're giving

And may we withhold any judgment un-real

'Til 'tis determined just how 'tis that they feel

Our prayer, 'tis that one day our barriers we'll withdraw

And ne'er accuse one of them, of being a scoff-law

Surrounded

When researching the origin of the word atmosphere

Early on, we find its exact meaning not too clear

We recognized it as a term related to the air

Then finally we assumed, as it seemed only fair

That how it derived under such nomenclature

'Twas simply the result of its ubiquitous nature

Amazing Grates
a.k.a. Time to Re-fuel

There lived this beloved lad named Alexander

Who hooked a big fish and did land her

More-over, he and grandpa would sit by the fireplace & gaze

At the fire with all of its captivating blaze

Thus when the logs burned low, 'twould be quite late

Grandpa would lean over & gently whisper, Alexander the Grate

Who's Counting?
a.k.a. Numerology Exploited
(Dedicated to Ron Schowengerdt and His Family)

1 Big Hello 2 U 4 Waterfordians

    'Twould be a 4-some if U4 played accordions

4 1 2 note, if 1 8 10 shrimp as of late

'Twould be 6 more than the 4 1 first 8

If 1 were 2 munch be 4 1 8

'Twould 10 2 tell just what 1 8

I've 1 thing 2 say, be 4 2 late

'Tis 2 wish U4 the best at 30728

Of course, as 2 1 rule of thumb

These numbers, all 10 can benumb

Peace, Progress, and Prosperity

When musing o'er Peace, Progress, and Prosperity

Many tho'ts come to mind with celerity

Reflecting on the many obstacles thru which we have been

We realize 'twas thru perseverance & courage we did win

Then another tho't looms as we make this confession

We have ne'er been those to abide our fellow-man's oppression

For we know full well thru our studied decision

That the world's complex society needs much revision

If we only would cooperate without reservation

And to Humanity's needs we'd give concentration

Then the dreams of the well-meaning would come to each nation

Despite all our efforts, we candidly make an admission

That much needs to be done, ere these ideals come to fruition

Having hope for the future should be our obsession

And we pray that we'll ne'er embrace retrogression

What Goes Around

When contemplating just what on earth we're to do
Living with all other humans and animals too
We may be prone to wonder just what is our lot
And if in our journey through life 'tis we forgot
Just what it is that constitutes brotherhood
And if we've done the good deeds that we should
Thus no matter be it an elephant or an elf
Unquestionably, one must begin with one's self

Blabber-Mouth

Unfortunately, there lived this loud mouth named Cryit
And his loud voice he was e'er wont to ply it
For when anyone else dared to make a suggestion
He'd adamantly yell out, it's out of the question
And ere this effrontery should become a steady diet
Why couldn't he shut up his big mouth & be quiet

Impulsiveness

Were I to be blessed with monetary reward
Permitting buying non-essentials that I could afford
'Twould be that we'd all be in one accord
For we'd acquiesce & join the rest of the horde

Naught E'er Thrown Away
a.k.a. Pack Rat

Thus, 'tis so oft' to myself that I've muttered
    How my home could have become so cluttered
In trying to explain I stammered and stuttered
And 'twas with total dismay that I shuddered

In A Stew

There were times and there were more than a few
I wondered when I last cooked my neighbor a stew
So I decided to cook and it was much to my relief
    For I knew he ne'er hesitated to give voice to a beef
And so, at last our beef stew was complete
And 'twas with relish and much gusto he'd eat
Had I not done this for my good friend Doc Bonner
I would otherwise have had to pay him honor

Take a Breather

In the event good news one were to report
Yet the impact of its full meaning fell short
We trust that most individuals would exhort
    And that the remaining populace would not snort

Music and Rhyme

Were I to be asked my most rhyme sublime
'Twould be the one that was most likely to chime
And could I but re-trace my actions in time
I'm sure they would naught but have improved my rhyme

What, No Erupt?

When standing outside, I found it warming up
    As the cold blasts of winter, they seemed to give-up
Tho' any rhyming, it may well tend to disrupt
I pray that this one, 'twill not be one to corrupt

Cold-Hot

After enduring the hardships of winter's cold blast
We're reminded of the many similar times in the past
When 'twas that the temperatures, they simply left us aghast
And needless to say, we thankfully welcomed summer at last

Humane Disdain

'Tis about man's myriad trials that I've perused
    And the count-less instances when he was abused
So let no one become complacent or confused
Be it known that his self-esteem was bruised.

Err Not in My Ear, I Pray
(Dedicated to Dr. Andrea Garrett)

Today, I visited Dean Clinic on a mission
That definitely ne'er pertained to nuclear fission
For this procedure I had made a considered decision
    Some time before Dr. Garrett would make her incision
Then just imagine my surprise and utter elation
When I was told 'twould only require radiation

Leprosy

'Twas one evening as I began to disrobe
Somehow my tho'ts turned to the minute microbe
An organism that's infinitely small
Nevertheless, 'tis capable of affecting us all
    Apprehensively, I started my own condition to probe
And 'twas then that I recalled that of hapless Jobe

The 4 J's
(Dedicated to My Granddaughter
& Great Grandchildren Jocelyn, Jackson, James David, & Jorgiana
Acuff)

I'm over-joyed to express that the 4 J's have it!

Should you not believe me, then just ask Dick Cavett

For if there are any that fail to savvy it

   Then they'd better think twice and get into the habit!

Alexander the Great II
(Dedicated to My Great Grandson Alexander Isaac Templin)

Here's to my Great Grandson Isaac Alexander

'Tis true, his journey thru life may meander

Although his accomplishments may cause some to gander

I'm confident that they'll ne'er encompass any slander

With Such a Friend, Who Needs Enemies

This friend of mine offered me a proposition
That needless to say was not without condition
The nature of his proposal was of such convolution
That in many ways I felt it a personal intrusion
He arrogantly asked me to fork over two grand
With an attitude, which, was more like a demand
In denying his request I hoped a lesson to teach
For his soul's salvation, his God he'll have to beseech

Wealth Defined

I've oft' wondered why 'tis we're not all wealthy
For 'tis true most are relatively healthy
The answer may well be one that is stealthy
After reviewing all our priorities and habits and such
We realize that the need for their revision is much
And if we pursue mediocrity, we'll remain in its clutch
However, if 'tis the welfare of our fellow-man we truly care
And we're motivated to help with all we can spare
Then the rewards of wealth, we'll surely more than share

Ask and Ye Shall Receive

'Twas as I sat by myself, hour by hour
Just waiting for some meaningful tho't to flower
That I was suddenly struck by tho'ts of His power
And His Infinite Grace, which o'er all does tower
I can only pray that for the errors of my way, to this hour
Some small measure of forgiveness He'll shower

May I

May I, without faltering, continue on with my rhyme

And may it somehow prove worth-while in time

May I find that the dreams of my youth are fulfilled

Ere the inexorable passage of time, it is stilled

May I, with humility, and without tho't of remuneration

Contribute what little I can to each nation

May I express a fervent hope, that 'tis Heaven we'll share

With all who've repented and accepted Jesus, who'll be there

May I with His guidance, His precepts understand

And may I, unquestionably, obey His every command

Tho'ts Asea

When sailing with my fellow-man on board

And providing him with comforts that I could afford

Now we all share dreams that we've e'er looked toward

'Twas just then I decided to put in fast forward

Realizing that with many aspects of life, we are bored

Yet, we're commanded to love one another, saith the Lord

Expectation
(Dedicated to Debra, Bethany, & Robyn Schowengerdt)

When confronted with the infinite nature of time
With all the mountains that there are to climb
And tho' 'tis my feeble efforts to write rhyme
    'Tis little compensation for their dedication and time
Yet someday we do pray that we'll review
All the plaudits that we may be entitled to

Let It Be

When searching in life for a bonus
I prayed that greed did not own us
Tho' 'tis that countless friends may disown us
    I fervently pray that no one will e'er clone us

The Ultimate Resource

There are many things in life that beset us
Most of which are inclined to upset us
    While allowing too many of these things to get us
We futilely wish that they had ne'er met us
So we continue to wend on life's way
Fulfilling our appointed role day by day
Hoping that our efforts conform to His way
Belatedly, should all else forsake us, we pray

Underworld

'Twas early one morning, as I left my lounge

I spied a wee ant who was wont to scrounge

Giving wonder to just how it was he was able

To collect enough food for his family table

Observing his endless trips which were so entire

    'Twas his industrious nature, one had to admire

Bullish or Bear

When re the stock market, one day I was thrashin'

And all the time hoping I wouldn't take a bashin'

After scanning Dow, NASDAQ, Standard & Poors

I couldn't decide whether to buy Miller or Coors

At one point, I tho't of those making jams & jellies

    And even gave consideration to the lowly sow bellies

'Twas that the markets' un-certainty & whip-lashin'

Finally compelled me a CD to cash in

Privacy

While considering the enormity of my verse

'Tis my hope they'll continue no worse

    And may-haps when you're sitting on the John

Hopefully, they'll not make all of you yawn

Life's Goal

Should we pause to reflect on the whole

The eternal disposition of one's soul

May God, knowing well that I'll try,

    His commandments with all Ten to comply

Ne'er Too Late
(Dedicated to My Deceased Wife
Mary Sanders Baird nee: Mary Ellen Hughes)

    When considering our contribution, there's a ton

Of all the things that we might have done

Tho' their fulfillment may be open to debate

Rest assured that it's ne'er too late

Above All

When our thoughts they are free in our mind
And we're striving to determine their kind
There's one that stands out above all
'Tis to hark for the voice of His call
Tho' we may be bewildered by life's turns
Yet inwardly, we all know our heart yearns
To respond fully to the Love in His call
For our Salvation depends on it Above All

Recognition

When I think of the events that befall
To the world and to one and us all
Tho' many in our view did appall
There were few that did truly enthrall
Now these events, which occur midst us all
They were ne'er at our beck-and-call
And thus so as to shorten this verse
We recognize events could have been much worse

Elder Thought

Now through moments, 'tis long that I've been
For this span, 'tis I should surely have ken
Of our world filled with its turmoil & clout
Just what it is, that it's all about

Please Don't Flunk Her

There once posed a Lady named Dunker
    And 'twould e'er be my last thought to debunk her
For 'tis on my knees I do prayerfully hunker
And pray that my verse 'twill ne'er be a clunker

Game-Seeker

(Dedicated to our Grandson, Richard William Schowengerdt)

The above title well applies to our grandson Rich

Who'd freely admit to this fact with ne'er a hitch

Tho' the love of hunting & fishing e'er within was ragin'

'Twould be hunting this day that he'd engage in

So on horse-back, thru many hills, sage-brush and valley

He'd travel more miles than one could e'er tally

As with all else, with ammo he was frugal

Thus, he'd hark for the elusive Elk's bugle

For this hunt, he might well have chosen a Luger

Yet 'twas wisely he relied on his trusty ole Ruger

Then finally the object of his quest appeared granted

He halted and perhaps somewhat inwardly panted*

*Now re this word, for sure 'tis applicable

I'll qualify with just three words, e'en tho' unflappable

Being One among many who'd ne'er use graffiti

Took dead aim and felled that trophy Wapiti

Gone Fishin'

The most disgusting fishing experience that I can relate
Was, after driving 50 miles to a remote area, I'd left my live bait
Now this lake I had chosen, after a diligent search
For it appeared to be one having both walleye & jumbo perch
My artificial lure had a propeller which was supposed to whirl
But after an hour of countless casts, the dang thing refused to twirl
About this time, I looked around & the Game Warden I did see
One who'd been watching me closely from behind an oak tree
The last thing that happened, which was by far the most harassing
I was fishing on private property & I got arrested for trespassing

Definitely

When 'tis that I humbly strive each day
His Loving thoughts, in some way, to relay
For despite all the words one might say
    We'll all know their true meaning, one day

High Hopes

I find it difficult to recall, as to just how many nights
That I've dreamt of my Dear Lord & those Heavenly sights
For my hope, it seemed as though 'twould e'er be
That a vision of Him holding my hand, I'd see

Broken Promises

When one thinks of life's promises & their fragility
The fulfillment of all, merely an exercise in futility
'Tis my sincere prayer, that while biding my time
I'll be granted the way, to give some meaning to my rhyme

Love is the Answer

Once again, as one thinks of one's sister or brother
One's reminded of His words, to love one another
One need only remember, this maxim so true
For that is all that's e'er been asked of you

Constant Motion

There once lived an incomparable athlete named Gunner
Who achieved indescribable renown as a runner
And lest the other activities in his life, we may tend to limit
'Twas that he was ne'er known to be idle, for one minute
For his countless cross-country runs, he was world-famous
'Twould be that any one of which would most certainly lame us,
While the answer to these remarkable feats, we're all sortering
'Tis one thing for sure, he'll ne'er be arrested for loitering

The Essence of Rhyme

When I think of all the great poets & writers of our time
Who have conveyed faultlessly, with words so sublime
For were it not for their priceless inspiration o'er time
I'd find myself ill-equipped, to give thought to my rhyme

A Lady's Choice

When a photographer, to a Lady, makes an improper suggestion
One that which truly poses a most serious question
Should she slap his sassy face for being so rude
Or should she just simply relent and pose for him nude

Nine Eleven

When it is that one attempts to define terrorism

One most likely, will classify it as sadism

Unless, of course, one delights in masochism

    If one were to speak of these, without making a sound

One would be the best damned ventriloquist around

I.O.U

When one muses o'er the many bills one must pay

That have e'er accrued relentlessly day to day

Tho' being somewhat late, in the payment of my installment

I'm sure that my creditor, was not overwhelmed with enthrallment

Love, Unbounded

When 'tis I've given thought to the immensity of life

And of its many foibles and errors that are rife

Yet despite all the discord and strife o'er time

I've striven to decipher & give some thought to my rhyme

There must be an answer for the world's benevolence & Love

And we find 'tis our Lord Jesus & His Father from above

His Infinite Love

Should one count the many millions on earth, who must
Place in Him, above all, their unconditional trust
For tho' one muddles o'er calculations and such
The Love of our God, far out-stretches one's touch

Eternity

When one dreams, in thoughts and reality
That life on earth is the finality
One must remember that our God up above
Has prepared a final haven, filled with His Infinite Love
For His Heaven, no matter one's earthly behavior
Awaits All who accept His Son Jesus as their Savior

Doubtless

If one should pause, to think of the many gifts from above
All of which must be attributed to His Infinite Love
For should we e'er be prone, His Love to doubt
Just think what we'd be like, His Love without

Marilyn
(Dedicated to Marilyn Larson)

Marilyn, my Marilyn, I could ne'er express enough thanks

For the immeasurable support, 'tis that yours ranks

'Tis that I've been privileged, many friends to know

As if this singular honor, He's seen fit to bestow

Again, Marilyn, my Marilyn, 'tis the theme of the Preakness Stakes

And my prayer for You & Yours, 'tis that misfortune ne'er o'er-takes

Grace

When 'tis that one, nearing the end, must face

The reality of life on earth and his place

Tho' one may have few virtues to embrace

One prays that our Dear Lord will erase

The faults and mis-directions in our life, without trace

    'Tis then we'll know the full thrust of His Infinite Grace

Misrepresentation

In London lived an astronomer named Loons

Who was e'er searching sky-ward for more moons

He was the subject of many editors' lampoons

For he also loved listening to all Looney-Tunes

Tho' many Londoners considered him quite daffy

He just continued to chew on his self-pulled taffy

As to UFO's, he claimed to have seen the biggest saucer

Then again, he emphatically claimed to be Geoffrey Chaucer

Low Life

While in this world we're occupied with this & that
We may tend to over-look the plight of the rat
One that scrounges for garbage, tidbits and such
And one whose struggle for existence has been much
Tho' he's somehow managed to survive, without our support
There's one thing for sure, he'll ne'er 'rat on' us in court

Revival

When I think of the many times that I've kissed
    And of the many more opportunities that I've missed
I've oft' wondered, just what would be the sensation
If one were to give, mouth to mouth resuscitation

Green Light

    Again when considering the transitory nature of life
And of one's destiny, which may loom so rife
There's no U-turn for the reversal of one's ways
Only a forward path that leaves record of one's days

Disparity

Tho' we ourselves are all most fortunate
    There are countless millions who are less fortunate
And lest one finds a cure for this disparity
One may be judged guilty of one's lack of charity

As the Twig is Bent
a.k.a. Shelter with Guidance
(Dedicated to Mr. John Furstenberg, his Staff,
and The Omaha Home for Boys)

When one thinks of those engaged in the betterment of mankind
'Tis my thought that's readily drawn to You and your kind
For 'tis through the selfless dedication of You and your Staff
That has deterred so many Boys from forming a gang's riff-raff
We all should be made aware, that one's pathway in youth
E'er leads to the fulfillment of one's dreams, in truth

Known Bestowal

When I think of the countless rhymes that I've written
'Tis that of their sheer volume that I'm smitten
For above all granted to me in my time
'Twould be my God-given talent to rhyme

Judgment

When one seeks in one's way to make amends
For the true accounting of all of their sins
And should one e'er strive their destiny to avoid
They'll find, at last, 'tis in the Hands of the Lord

Finality

When, on earth, one nears the end of one's days
And 'tis that all's left up to Him who assays
One need not dwell on the error of one's ways
For 'tis YOUR FORGIVENESS for them, that one prays

Repentance

When in life one attempts one's purpose to explain
One prays that one's efforts, have not all been in vain
And tho' 'tis that HIS message of LOVE is GOD-sent
'Tis that, of our transgressions, we must repent

Just In Time

When 'twas one day that I became involved
In a discussion that appeared to be unresolved
Then perhaps due to the uncertainty of fate
    The answer came to us all, fortunately not too late

Grant

Once again, when one considers the passage of time
And to the ultimate heights that one might climb
    For 'tis through my God and HIS SON JESUS so sublime
That I've been permitted to write my humble rhyme

Enigma

    Though 'tis that life's ladder I've e'er striven to climb
I found that its answers, 'twas that of mine
And I wonder, just what it has been, in time
That has contributed to the work of my rhyme

Friend

When trying to evaluate the worth of a Friend
We find that such values are all without end
For of all life's society, with which we contend
    There's naught to compare with that of a True Friend

Non Al Dente

There lived an older man named John Booth
Who married an elderly widow named Ruth
Now, his middle name was not Wilkes, in truth
'Tho mild-mannered, at times, he was somewhat uncouth
His wife's culinary out-put, he gulped down e'en tho' toothless
Yet sadly, upon her expiration, 'twas when he became Ruthless

Depth of Song

When our thoughts they are definitely wandering
And our minds, they are given to pondering
'Tis when considering our souls and the hereafter
That we'll sing praises to God from the rafter

Life's Quest

Initially, I assure you, I'd be the last to suggest
Being capable of defining the scope of Life's Quest
For our many differences in life, they do vary
Coping with its unknown & pit-falls, we need to be wary
And so finally, we realize that our true Quest in Life
Notwithstanding all of its turmoil and strife
Must inevitably point to One's Eternal Life

Feline Ferocity

Note: As a matter of record,
the following verse was done entirely from scratch

In London lived two cats, named Murmur & Purr
Who were both constantly preening their fur
And being quite content where they were
They usually were not prone to stir

Now comes the English Bulldog named Drool
Whose jowls, they o'er-lapped every rule
And, in all modesty, considered himself quite cool
Having come from a kennel in East Liverpool
'Twas thus that Drool decided he'd like to munch
On the cats' most favored light tuna lunch

Suddenly, as we watched the scenario unfold
All hell broke loose 'round that light tuna bowl
Now Drool, 'tho having had countless alley fights & spats
Had ne'er met the likes of these Two Calico Cats

The Meaning of Family
(Dedicated to the Schowengerdts)

In an effort to avoid giving a homily

I'll strive to give some meaning to family

With my thoughts and with tongue-in-cheek

Give some expression, both humble and meek

'Tho some may look on life as a lottery

We know that it's truly camaraderie

Be assured that naught in life can e'er efface

The Love of our God and His Infinite Grace

Again, while seeking for Family's true meaning

    'Tis toward Love and To-Gether-Ness I'm leaning

    For the many occasions when we all joined ranks

    Those times together, 'tis we give endless thanks

For those days as we all do well know

And for the many times we've enjoyed al-fresco

The answer, which may only come from above

For the step-side of my family I also love

Carry On

When 'tis that one, o'er the term of life's stretch

Some little element of you, one will be allowed to be-fetch

For though growing older, 'tis e'er then a matter of fact

We pray that one's demise, 'twill ne'er e'er impact

Indolence

Now this lazy man, trying to decide the fewest
Of the many disdainful tasks that he'd doest
He chose to slough off, for in addition he must
Cope with all of his indolence, lechery, and lust
    And ere we lose the meaning of this verse's full thrust
'Twas we just threw up our hands in disgust

Aerial Supremacy

'Twas one Sunday morn, as I was just leaving church
That I spied a lone blue jay sitting on his perch
He seemed somewhat uneasy & emitted a raucous squawk
With his eyes pointed skyward on a soaring hawk
'Twas then that the tho't came to me, as I passed on by
Just what our world would be like, if man could fly

Equality

When it is that we'll all meet our God face to face
    And if we've lived amiably together, regardless of race
Then if 'tis that we've put Self in last place
We'll be the recipient of His Infinite Grace

Let It Be Heard

When considering its sound and its size
We are finally compelled to realize
    That the human voice is the greatest instrument
That can e'er be measured by any increment

Be Thankful

And so 'tis, as we proceed with our walk
That we reveal many tho'ts during our talk
'Tho at times we feel we should rightfully balk
    'Tis that we've had very little reason to squawk

An Individual

    Now when our fellowman we attempt to review
And the true purpose of his life to construe
We find there is really little that we knew
So we'll just cap it off, with Who's Who

Priorities Askew

There lived a man named Moran who was wayward
For 'twas the pleasures in life that he favored
And 'tho he seldom found these to be savored
'Twas toward this end that he doggedly labored

Divine Contribution

Now our God, knowing well that His gift 'twould please us
'Twas that He sent His Beloved Son Our Lord Jesus
And in reflecting on His countless other gifts from above
Surely none can compare with the gift of His Love

Acknowledgment

When questioning the writing of Rhyme, as I should
'Twas then that my Dear Lord said I could
So I set forth to pen random verse
Fully aware 'twould be for better or worse

Now after penning verse, 'tis upon reflection
That my Rhyming has e'er continued under His direction
And had it not been for His presence close by
The writing of Rhyme, I might have failed to try

To Lucy and Her Choir
(Dedicated to Lucy Sandy – Director of Fontana, WI
Community Church choir (U.C.C.)

First of all, there is naught but to admire

The dedication that you've shown to your choir

'Tho at times the choir could use more voices

Those times are ne'er ones that are by choices

For when we all sing freely and rejoice

Everyone knows that we've giv'n sound to His voice

Restraint Required
a.k.a. The Dearth of Girth or For What It's Worth

Should you e'er feel a touch of avarice or greed

And you decide 'tis of life's fullest you'll feed

"Tho you pile your plate high with calories

Not at all commensurate with your salaries

You must realize that ere it's too late

One need not necessarily empty their plate

Bombs Away

'Tho the earth is constantly faced with erosion
    All fear the destruction of an ultimate explosion
Yet despite all of our outward aplomb
Were we e'er to have triggered the Big Bomb
The dire result, all the way from London to Laos
Unavoidably, would be one of absolute chaos

Blunt Introduction

I once knew a fellow named Rude
'Twas e'er his wont to intrude
When asked why his actions were crude
    Merely said that his first name was Rude

An Ode on Brotherhood
(Dedicated to my brother, Bascom Griffith Baird)

Were I to be giv'n my 'druthers

I'd rather be a friend to my Brothers

To love them must e'er be a plus

For they live on this earth, just like us

Now, no matter what lays in our path

    For we all hope to evade God's wrath

E'en tho' there's little we know of His plan

May we ne'er forget our fellow-man

Descendants

When one thinks of one's descendants & ranks
One is compelled to give of endless thanks
Tho' one must leave the outcome to chance
'Tis that I'll e'er strive, their future to enhance

Academics Gone Astray

When 'tis that one is inclined to define diversity
One must include all of one's dealings with adversity
And tho' 'twas that one was schooled at a University
Regrettably, 'twas that all ended up in perversity

Bounty

When 'tis that one finds one's self in a clutch
And, in all honesty, in need of a crutch
For tho' we may proclaim with anger and such
May we ne'er forget that our life has been much

Weep Not

May we ne'er weep o'er that we can't change
Or e'er strive the inevitable to re-arrange
Just be thankful that our God above knows
Of all the rightful paths in life that we chose
    Then at night, when one lies down on one's pillow
'Tis that one need ne'er weep, as does the willow

No Need to Grieve

Were it e'er that I was required to retrieve
    From an action that one could scarcely conceive
Tho' the most I could expect was a reprieve
I'd still pray for my Lord's pardon, and believe

Seeking

    Should it be that one's in search of true love
And seeking an answer from Him up above
Were it not for His Love and His Grace
A gift which all other queries, does erase

Calvary

When thinking of Him and His crown of thorn
'Twas that all vestiges of sin were shorn
And tho' 'tis that it's more difficult to trace
The full extent of His Love and His Grace

Do You Dig It?

'Twas in time past, there lived a miner named Higgins
Who spent virtually all of his time at his diggin's
'Twas with gold nuggets, he had hoped to fill his box
Yet all he'd e'er dug up, was earthworms & rocks
Lately, when tested for sanity & his countless bloopers
He was found to be nuttier than a big jar of goobers

Tip-Toe
(Dedicated to my Great Grand-daughter
Briar Rose Aurora Templin)

Here's to the one and only Briar Rose
Who moves both lithely and nimbly as she goes
And so 'tis that while one is seeking an answer
She may well become, an artistic toe-dancer

Grandson
(Dedicated to my Grandson James Spencer Templin)

Were I e'er asked, what is my opinion or more

Re my Grandson Spence, I will freely explore

    May our precious Lord Jesus, hold his hand e'er more

And e'er continue all of his poetic works, to shore

Al Fresco

There lived this couple named Harry & Heather

Who, this day, decided to eat out in nice weather

    During lunch, a fierce argument ensued between them

And naught could placate either her or him

Heather lunged at Harry & Harry lunged at Heather

And so 'twas thus, that they had lunge together

No Greater Love

Again, when one ponders o'er the many gifts from above

One is faced with the reality of His Infinite Love

For 'tis in our lives, as one surely must know

That 'tis that No Greater Love, that one can bestow

Greater Love Hath No Man or Woman
aka The Ultimate Contribution

Here's a tribute to all our military personnel

Who've striven so valiantly, oppression to repel

From the very beginning and Old Bunker Hill

They've been engaged in conflicts that plague us still

From the shores of Iwo Jima, Okinawa & all the way to Iraq

They've given selflessly, knowing not when or if they'd be back

Now, as thousands return past their homeland border

All too many suffer from Post-Traumatic Stress Disorder

May we offer all acclamations, which they so richly deserve

For 'tis for Freedom &our way of life, they fight & die to preserve

May Good Fortune E'er Attend Ya

I was asked to write a rhyme about Lucinda

Who lived all alone in a quaint hacienda

Located in Wisconsin, on the outskirts of Zenda

    Now, should these lines e'er happen to offend ya

'Tis a sincere apology that I'll sure send ya

    And more-over, a large hanky to cry in, I'll lend ya

Briar Rose

(Dedicated to my Great Grand-daughter
Briar Rose Aurora Templin)

Should I e'er attempt a rhyme for Briar Rose

'Twould sorely test my capacity to compose

For we're confident that her life as she grows

Will be filled with virtues untold & all else one can dispose

May our Loving Lord Jesus, attend her closely always

And e'er be beside her, through-out the length of her days

No. 4
A Tribute to an Inimitable Quarterback

Here's to the athlete wearing 4 in green and gold

Whose performance conforms to no other one's mold

For there were e'er few in Lambeau Field who knew just how hard he

Strove to carry on the tradition set by Legend Vince Lombardi

Of course, 'tis none other than our one and only Brett Favre

Who, if in Europe, might have to speak French in Le Havre

While we're rapt with the grid-iron mastery of this awesome survivor

He drills yet another T.D. pass to his favorite target Don Driver

And then, during execution of their famed Lambeau Leap

The warm & frenzied appreciation of their Fans they do reap

For the T.V. watchers, not in attendance, yet staunch Packer Backers

I sincerely hope that your reception encountered no Hackers

In the Beginning

When reflecting on the Creation of Life and our World
The Infinite nature of it All becomes unfurled
For since the Beginning and o'er the vastness of time
    There has reigned One, both Omnipotent and Sublime
Down thru the Ages, we find ones He ne'er chose
    Regrettably, there e'er has been and will e'er be those
Consumed by Ego and unwillingness to repent
    Seemingly unaware 'twas why His Son Jesus was sent

Why

Why is it that we so oft' wonder
    Why our life has its error and blunder
And why is it that we so oft' partake
    Of both its misadventure and mistake
    When we strive to connect such a link
We realize that we had only to think

Aspiration

When aspiring for life's ultimate goal
Of course, 'tis the salvation of one's soul
And yet, in our lives in between
Lay obstacles that may be unseen
So thus, no matter how the dice may roll
    We know when we've accomplished our goal

James L. Baird

A Horse Player's Lament

When attending one day at Twin Spires

I decided to just play Early Fires

'Tho his odds in this race were quite long

He did appeal to several in the throng

Yet, despite all Early's efforts to dispose

    'Twas the favorite, who prevailed by a nose

Judgment Day

    At this time, if there's one tho't that should seize us

'Twould be the birth of our Blessed Lord Jesus

Who was sent by His Father from above

To assure all mankind of His Love

Though Jesus met with many tribulations

The power of His Father's Love reached all nations

And ere that we reach our world's end

Hopefully, any flaws in our souls we'll amend

Recovery Assured
(Dedicated to Dr. Stanley W. Gruhn)

Our prayers for you are both contrite & earnest

For you're one of our world's fore-most Internists

    Again, we pray to our Grace-filled God on bended knee

That an even more productive future, you'll live to see

Dedication
a.k.a. Relentless Resolve
(Dedicated to President George W. Bush)

'Tis heartening to see that things are looking up
    And 'tis long overdue that this world it did wake up
For it has long been to me quite clear
That your direction for All has e'er been sincere
As to those virtues and values we all hold so dear

Devotees of Rhyme

'Tis my verse, for all those I well knew
    Took the time, 'tho their spare moments were few
Its meaning and thoughts to review
Hopefully, 'tis that they chose not to eschew

All Too Brief

    Once again, when considering the Brevity of Life
Filled with both its glory and strife
'Tho in Life, we encounter praise and scorn
We fully realize as each new day is born
That 'tis a fact, after all's said and done
Seemingly, 'tis o'er ere 'twas hardly begun

James L. Baird

Holiday Greetings

Dear Relatives & Friends One and All:

I wish a Merry Xmas to both short & tall

And from the sky, which hovers o'er us all

May Ole Santa's laden sleigh ne'er fall

Should it happen with a crash & much noise

Just imagine the loss of gifts and toys

That were meant for all good girls & boys

Thus thwarting all their anticipation & joys

The presents, Ms Santa & her half dozen Elves

Had so lovingly packed from the shelves

    'Twas their leader Ole Rudolph, the Red Nosed One

Who this trip, simply forgot how to run

And 'tis sadly a fact, after all's said & done

He caused Ole Santa's disastrous Last Run

On Donner, Blitzen & All the Reindeer

Am wishing for All, a rewarding New Year

Self-Awakening

If in Life, we've done the best that we can
    And we've e'er treated kindly our fellowman
Hopefully, ere we're judged by Him up above
We will have learned of His Infinite Love
And after reviewing all the things we hold dear
The reason for our Being, 'twill be made clear

Contriteness

This subject, 'tis somewhat difficult to assess
Yet 'tis one we sooner or later need address
When in meditation and in all humbleness
In all our lives, there comes a time to confess
That in fulfillment of His Word, we've fallen short
For all too often, worldly pleasures we exhort

    Now 'tis nigh impossible for we earthly ones to conceive
Of the countless Blessings which from Him we receive
And should we e'er depart from His Love and His Grace
My prayer 'tis we'll return ere we meet face-to-face

Allegiance Unbounded
a.k.a. Flander's Field Revisited

When we pause to remember all those lost in War

We are hard pressed to recall just what it was for

For rivalries and unrest still exist to this day

And Freedom from oppression appears light years away

To achieve Equality & Brotherhood, we have a long way to go

'Tho these were more virtues for which our Fallen Heroes fought so

We reverently pray for all conflict to cease

And may the Tribute o'er their graves, e'er read R.I.P.

Trail's End

When one day, my mood it was moping

And to elevate my spirits I was groping

I hoped to write something bright and cheerful

And most certainly, nothing rash or fearful

Despite all efforts to write something upbeat

My lines only seemed each effort to defeat

    After walking many miles which I found provoking

    I just decided to give my tired feet a good soaking

Soup's On
a.k.a. No Carry Outs – Please or Nothing to Go

Ere starting our dinner, 'twas we wanted to be helpful
    We planned a menu that would be both tasty & healthful
We prepared a beef roast, for much protein 'tis rich in
And from the veggies, we'd clean away any lichen
If 'tis to avoid the heat of cookin' you're itchin'
Then 'tis you need only to get outta the kitchen

Personal Cognizance

    Now 'tis long I've been addicted to verse
For to rhyme, I need ne'er to rehearse
'Tis to all of these lyrics in time
I'll devote all the talent that is mine

Incorrigibility
a.k.a. Retribution

When being confronted with the downside of man

We come face-to-face with all the ignoble acts he can

Though unwarranted, inflict on his fellowman

This evil man, his life filled with injustices and greed

Did ne'er e'er one iota of morality heed

He'd be both envious & jealous of those who'd succeed

He'd delight in saying things demeaning & denigrating

Add to this, an attitude one could barely keep from hating

In summation, there's very little more we can say

For we know he'll reap his deserved fate on Doom's Day

A Yearly Routine

We annually face Winter, as we go to and fro

A season accompanied by much cold and snow

We strive to keep warm and perform our tasks

And comply with the demands that living asks

   'Tis soon that Spring arrives, and there is no more snow

'Tis then that Ole Santa, his three gardens does grow

'Tis that he does this on purpose, so he can Ho-Ho-Ho

Dawn to Dusk

Seemingly, it has been since the day we were born
That we've e'er marveled at the dawning of morn
With the warmth & brightening rays of the rising Sun
We give thanks that once more a new day has begun
    Hopefully, 'twill be a day filled with Love & Good Deed
    And the giving of special care to our fellowman's need
And ere the twilight of each day does befall
One will resign to the sheer ecstasy of it all

'Till Death Do Us Part

'Twas a wedding late one afternoon in June
As all harked to the sound of the Lohengrin's tune
Parents, grandparents, & other relatives of course
Were all in attendance, holding front center in full force
Now comes the Father & Bride resplendent in white
And the familiar processional was going just right
The Groom and His Best Man were waiting this while
Then the sight of his Bride-to-be brought forth a smile
However, the Groom appeared somewhat wan and strange
As if with his Best Man's position, he'd like to exchange
Lately, his Brothers, Cousins & not a few smarties
Had nearly done him in with their Bachelor parties
Wanting to show tokens of their kinship & love
They had plied him full of Spirits not sent from above
Finally, with visions of Honeymoon filling his head
He was asked if his Betrothed he'd now wed
And 'twas a meek and submissive 'I do' he said

Procrastination
a.k.a. Better Late than Never

"Twas most recently in matter of time
    The Lord placed his hand gently on mine
Saying My Son James, 'tis now time
That you should continue to rhyme

The Dieter's Dilemma

Here's a regimen for just what 'tis worth
Were there tons of less fat on this earth
And to Veggies we'd turn from the turf
    Of excess calories there'd soon be a dearth
Which contribute so much to our girth

Prayer Answered

My prayer had e'er been that I'd sleep
Hopefully all His commandments to keep
For it was e'er that I tossed and I turned
'Twas for solace and slumber I yearned

Again, while restlessly turning in bed
My Lord spoke to me and He said
With a voice that pierced my Being so deep
    'Rest assured that this one night you'll sleep'

Quiet Please

There lived a lady orator named LeMaster
    Who'd shout, no matter what one asked her
So thus, to avert total disaster
We stuffed her Big Mouth full of plaster

A Paternal Reflection
(Dedicated to my son, James Leslie Baird)

'Twas recently and solely on whim
I recalled of days with my Son Jim
Those days, too infrequently they were
Yet in feelings, they created a stir
For such is the Love 'twixt we two
    That we ne'er were apart, <u>that</u> we knew

Introspection

While sitting alone with my thought
I recalled many things that I ought
To have done long before I did
Their importance to me 'twas hid
May Our God in His Infinite Grace
    My transgressions somewhat to erase

Decision
a.k.a. Recognition

Here's to President George W. Bush
And his lovely wife Laura Bush
Who'd ne'er give quarters in a push
'Twixt the two of them, they do so care
To better all our world and repair
All the wounds that war has left there
And so, ere we be-cloud our visions,
Hopefully, not to make many revisions
    May Our God guide you in your current decisions
Our prayer is that history we'll scan
Says for us all that you've been quite a Man

Soul Searching

    While searching for one word to rhyme
With the Love of our God, so sublime
I yearned to say just what was right
Aware of the magnitude of His Might
So with guidance from Him up above
I was assured of His ne'er-ending Love
'Tis to Him, we'll all answer at last
When our Life on this earth, it is past

Cpl Don Hillard – 24th Infantry – US Army
A Poetic Tribute

While attempting to determine the price

Involved with the true meaning of 'Sacrifice'

My finding thru the research I'd scan

'Tis that 'Greater Love Hath No Man'

'Tho wars may continue in this world

We pray more of its Unsung Heroes are Herald

    And may 'All Honors of Appreciation' be pillared

In memory of Our Service Man, Don Hillard

Denigration
a.k.a. Don't Call US – We'll Call You

    Unfortunately, there lived a ruffian named Maul

Who all those around him did appall

When to another a name he did call

A name that is loathed by us all

When this ill-side of him was shown

Our angst toward him was made known

Expectations 'Low-For' A championship
a.k.a. Ne'er a Meet Won

There lived a track team runner named Rofer

Whose pace more resembled that of a loafer

Quite unlike the well known speed of the gopher

Asked why a Championship his team did ne'er go-for

    Invariably replied that his team record 'twas e'er 0-for

Dream Realized

While attempting our family future to explore

Our prayers and dreams would e'er be for

Our children to be Those who when grown

    Their achievements in Life would make known

    Those talents which they inherently possessed

As to their precocity, 'twas e'er I had guessed

A Horse Lover's Confession
a.k.a. Shades of Damon Runyon

'Tis so oft' that I consider myself lucky

To have grown up in Georgetown, Kentucky

A region where the 'Bluegrass' does flourish

On which, 'tis ideal for all horses to nourish

My match-less Dad Lewis and Brother Grif

'Tho we rarely, if ever, had a tiff

We needed only to travel 10 mile

For standard-bred racing at Red Mile

To 'Louville' & 'The Kentucky Derby' we'd go

A race which all the world does love so

And then again, we'd give in to our weakness

By wagering on the historic 'Preakness'

Lastly, while e'er striving to avoid mistakes

    'Twas that we'd all bet on the 'Belmont Stakes'

'Tho some might frown on such speculation

We felt we'd done no harm to 'Our Nation'

Destiny

At the moment when I clearly could sense

The magnitude of Our God's Omnipotence

    Then came thoughts of the world's sham & pretense

Which must be considered by Him an offense

For 'tis we entered this world wholly bare

And 'tis naught that we'll take with us 'There'

The Reality of War
a.k.a. What Price Victory

With the ill-treatment of Humanity rife

And it seems all is dissension and strife

We face the value of ONE human life

For it has e'er been our lot, thus far

    To have been part of its bloodshed and scar

'Tis the hope of all those who care

That the scope of all modern warfare

'Twill ne'er expand beyond all repair

May the future, from a guidance unseen

Provide Peace and Harmony more serene

Finally, the countless Lives lost or maimed

Fortunately, <u>That</u> will ne'er be declaimed

Underground Renowned
a.k.a. The Biblical Flood
(Dedicated to Matt, Cindy, and Christina)

'Twas long ago that I should 'sorter'

Have known of the ground-swell of water

For ere the world was put on alert

'Twas long known by our Matt Schowengerdt

Now when measuring or calculating all of this rain

The answer may well be one that is plain

'Tho many tales of Mt. Ararat do abound

Sure 'tis Ole Noah and his Ark ran aground

Ere We Rush to Judgment
a.k.a. Think It Over

While reflecting on our fellow-man

And the many centuries that this does span

When considering his many hardships and woes

'Tis that that 'tis he alone knows

We pray no Rush to Judgment ensues

'Til we've walked some miles in his shoes

A Real No-Brainer

'Tho I've encountered many intellectuals in my time

'Twas this One that seemed to thwart all rhyme

For lacking in perception, he was not

Yet otherwise, he appeared to be a robot

Now surgeons, trying to determine how sick

Performed a lobotomy, which proved just the trick

'Tho a few may find my effort a classic mark

    For most, I'm sure 'twill ne'er approach 'Jurassic Park'

Priorities Aligned

'Tis more verse, as you might well expect

    Yet 'tis on my meaning that I hope you'll reflect

    Now many things in Life can prompt wanderlust

Much like the well-known 'California or Bust'

Yet, ere pursuing this new path, as we must

'Tis in Him, that we'll All stake our trust

Rhyme

When I think of all the rhymes I could write

    And of their meanings, 'tis true that I might

Fail to give credit to my God up above

    Who o'er me has e'er shed His Infinite Love

For 'tis thru His gift of my talent to rhyme

That I will, hopefully, understand o'er time

Bide-a-Spell

When one day, I was just passing through
I met a Dear Friend I once knew
I asked him to please Bide-a-spell
For these thoughts only to You I will tell
When we look back on our journey through Life
One can recall many thoughts that were rife
'Tho material things they were surely a bonus
Our sincere hope 'tis that they ne'er did own us
For our lives they are all too brief at best
'Tis we may tend to forget all the rest
For 'tis our Family and Children we well know
They're the Ones that we dearly love so
Yet, ere the twilight of Life it is spent
'Twas to persuade all man-kind to repent
That His Only Begotten Son He sent
Acceptance of Him, forgiveness does relent
    And again, the most precious gift He well meant
'Twas the priceless gift of His Son that He sent
And so, my Dear Friend, that is why
As we both found ourselves passing by
This message, I desired only You to tell
'Twas why I asked You to please Bide-a-Spell

Play Ball
a.k.a. Batter Up

Please note that the above means virtually the same

When one is referring to our National Game

An ideal day, 'tis that one should remark

On a World Series game to embark

Our Flag, it waved high in the breeze

'Tho the Fans seemed a tad ill-at-ease

Yet their zeal was apparent, should one hark

'Twas to be a special day at the Ole Ball Park

Uncharacteristically, the head Umpire was a Lady named Hall

Who, in a soprano-like tone, suddenly yelled 'Play Ball'

Which was met with great applause by us all

Now the Pitcher, who was both sinewy and lank

Did from the out-set, appear somewhat rank

And the first Batter who stepped into the box

Could have worn either White or Red Sox

Then the Pitcher fired a fast-ball to the plate

But the Batter's swing 'twas much too late

Now perhaps due to the first pitch and all

The Catcher's mitt somehow only tipped the ball

Further, despite all of the efforts to protect her

That fast-ball drilled Hall's chest protector

Regrettably, after a thorough check by the Medic & all

'Twas an exit for the Lady Umpire named Hall

Then as soon as a new head Umpire they did muster

He immediately cleaned off home-plate with his duster

Once this new head Umpire resumed the call

The Batter seemingly hit a fair ball

Yet despite all of his slide and his pace

He was narrowly called 'Out' at first base

As was expected, the offenses' rage caught on fire

And their manager kicked dirt on the First Base Umpire

For such was the intensity of his ire

That he hurled many epithets at this Umpire

During ejection, his last in this litany of derision

Definitely pertained to this Ump's lack of vision

Now 'twas back in the stands all this while

That the vendors, they worked every aisle

Hawking their Red-Hots, Colas and Cold Beers

The latter, 'twas that many over-drank of I fear

The home team, down 0 to 3, had many with dismay on their faces

Finally, at last in the sixth, 'twas that they loaded all bases

At this point, the manager elected to use a pinch-hitter

Affectionately known to one and all as 'Big Hitter'

Now Big-Hitter, 'twas a task he well knew

As from the dugout bat- rack he drew

His oft' used and beloved 'Louville Slugger'

Then to the Batter's box he did carefully lug her

With the Pitcher's first fast-ball, such clout he did 'bond'

He drove that baby o'er the centerfield wall and beyond

So Big Hitter, 'midst thunderous applause from the crowd

Completed the circuit, taking all the time that's allowed

For the Homer he cranked out, followed by his jubilant jog

Had well managed all four bases to un-clog

As the seventh inning stretch fans were taking

Much home team strategy was in the making

'Tho relying on defense was considered a trifle

All finally agreed on the visitors' offense to stifle

Now our home team manager had an Ace up his sleeve

He was confident he had just the Closer to relieve

Thus without any further hesitation or fidget

He signaled the bullpen for his seldom used Midget

'Tho his off-speed and fast-ball pitches did annoy some

The side-arm delivery of his curve was simply awesome

And notwithstanding his size and his stature

This day, he really 'brought it home' to the catcher

Leaving no doubt that with power & finesse he could throw

By retiring the next 9 batters in a row!

P.S. While aware you may not find this a gem

At least you'll know that I've tried – Just Jim

An Unique Individual
(Dedicated to Dr. John Harold Bonner DVM)

'Twas some years ago, a residence I was cravin'

When, through good fortune, I found Elderhaven

Here, I first had the great pleasure to meet

The One, who thru verse, I feel privileged to treat

And for those, who may not know the One I do honor

'Tis none other than our respected Vet Doc Bonner

And, luckily for All, Doc was born in Milburn, Illinois

And grew up near their Old Heritage farm as a boy

'Tho his peers chose to pursue careers mostly agrarian

Doc, due to an earlier incident, elected to become a Veterinarian

Now to select the best school posed a quandary

That o'er many days and nights, did ponder he

Then through myriad inquiries and much bicycle travel

The answer to this dilemma, he did finally un-ravel

For 'twas East Lansing that proved his quest to abate

Receiving his well-earned DVM from Mich St

Now Doc, to his Medics, by his first name 'John' he's known best

But 'tis by his middle name 'Harold' he's best known by the rest

So 'John Harold,' for organization, dedication, and hard work

Has ne'er been known from these qualities to shirk

From early on, when his animal clinic came to be

'Twould be his wont to practice true husbandry

And needless to say, with all known ethical codes he'd comply

For to all, his professional expertise he'd supply

And yet, for all those treated, 'tis my feeling somehow

His preference leaned towards those with a feline purr & meow

And so, Dr. John Harold Bonner, my Dear Friend

My prayer, 'tis that our association 'twill ne'er end

And lastly, to borrow from Edgar Allen Poe and his raven

Evermore, to enjoy our relation at your Elderhaven

The Joy-Hood of Youth

When speaking of the Joy-Hood of Youth
We feel compelled to tell only the truth
The carnival and circus they loved so
For 'twas e'er that they wanted to go
The Ferris Wheel lifted them up high
Where all beneath them met their eye
And the sight of their name brought a gleam
When stamped out on the Name-Tag machine
Perhaps not yet aware of the symbol of Dove
They glided gleefully thru the Tunnel of Love
Popcorn, Balloons & Hotdogs, their spirits did heighten
Yet 'tis true that the Ghost House did frighten
We saw many midgets as we all were bent
On the security of our seats in the Big Tent
What fun to sit by the Circus Three Rings
And watch all the animals, trainers, & things
And all the aerialists, who seemed to have wings
Yet 'twas the antics of the clowns
That did the most to erase any frowns
Surely, nothing in child-hood could be found
To beat riding up and down on the 'Merry-Go-Round'
In former days, we had not only The Parade
But also, the ever popular Penny Arcade
Besides peanuts & cracker-jacks, I recall one other dandy
'Twas when we all chewed on our pink cotton candy

Threads

'Twas once that I met a tailor named Mose

Who made many different styles of clothes

'Tho widely known for the way he sews

The secret of his patterns, he'd ne'er disclose

Though a few felt his styles somewhat grim

Most found that they were stylish and trim

    And ere by his making of clothes we judge him

Just think what we'd look like without them!

Self-Appraisal

In my dreams, there've been times ere I wake up

I've dreamt of analyzing my own personal make-up

Tho' to some I may present myself as a WIT, so I might

To all others, 'twill e'er be deemed that they're only HALF right

From Me to You

Sometimes when you note at your leisure

A trinket or keepsake you treasure

That regardless of how you may measure

    Just remember that it's all been my pleasure

Sincerely Yours

Now my friends, ere penning a closing Amen

For my prayer 'tis long it has been

    That any misfortune occurring in your future

'Twill require only a very small suture

Respectfully Yours,

James L. Baird

The Quintessential Rhymer

CPSIA information can be obtained at www.ICGtesting.com
Printed in the USA
LVOW060324030212

266710LV00001B/18/P